This book may be kept

# FOURTEEN DAYS

A fine will be charged for each day the book is kept overtime.

| JA 11 08 | | | |
|---|---|---|---|
| | | | |
| | | | |
| | | | |
| | | | |
| | | | |
| | | | |
| | | | |
| | | | |
| | | | |
| | | | |
| | | | |
| | | | |
| | | | |
| | | | |
| | | | |
| GAYLORD 142 | | | PRINTED IN U.S.A. |

# KNOWLEDGE
## OF
# THE EVENING

# KNOWLEDGE
# OF
# THE EVENING

*Poems 1950-1960*

*John Frederick Nims*

NEW BRUNSWICK, N.J.

RUTGERS UNIVERSITY PRESS

A number of the poems in this volume have
appeared previously and are reprinted by per-
mission of the following journals: *Botteghe
Oscure, Commonweal, Galleria, New World
Writing, Nuova Corrente, Poetry, Prairie
Schooner, Sewanee Review, The Times Liter-
ary Supplement* (London), *The Virginia
Quarterly Review. Christmas Ballad* is re-
printed from *The Poems of St. John of the
Cross* (Grove Press, 1959).

# CONTENTS

## I

## II

## III

## IV

## V

## VI

## VII

Gocémonos, Amado,
y vámonos a ver en tu hermosura
al monte y al collado,
do mana el agua pura;
entremos más adentro en la espesura.

. . . *al collado*: esto es, a la noticia vespertina,
que es sabiduría de Dios en sus criaturas y
obras y ordenaciones admirables; la cual es
aquí significada por *el collado*, por cuanto es
más baja sabiduría que la matutina.

# I

*Noi che tignemmo il mondo*
*di sanguigno*

# THE LOVER

The lover of many women in his time
Came to his time: the lap of earth uncloses.
"The true to none?"—with sorrow—"true to none
In the long handsome June of all my roses?"

The lover, faint with pain (death's nuclear flash
Had bared the chambers of his life before him,
Seedy resort hotel with two walls gone,
Beds on all fours and trailing laundry) bore him

Like one assured of sympathy—his ear
So cunning in all cadence of surrender.
His famous smile, the "eternal boy's," began;
His famous wistful shrug. The tone less tender:

"Much from an ancient fate. But not your doom.
Your doom is your conceit of what you are.
Violet-stained, in a white fire of lenses,
Your heart become its will: the cancerous star."

His hell began, a hissing of cold foliage.
Hell too much like Eden. A second glance
Showed in the brush a thousand Eves coquetting—
The country club on nights of the spring dance

Had such mysterious tussle in the shrubbery,
Ruby on velvet hushed, from owl to lark.
But here light hugged the turf, a lunar neon
Of taverns known. A thousand brows were dark.

The enchanted wood exhaling fogs of brandy:
Breasts candlelit, a dream of altars, swim.
Knees like the noble jewels that shaft a chalice.
And cloth of gold about the seraphim.

Fingers beckoning like hands on harpstrings.
Shoulders that ebb consenting. Sweetness choked
His heart in the old vice; he fell sobbing
"Thank God!"—the words sprung jackknives in his throat.

Two ankles shone like lotus; he flopped toward them
—Half-blinded seal—and spangled them with kisses.
And so kissed up and up in a long whinny
And shivered as he prayed and all delicious.

Kissed to the pulsing throat. Then knew his hell.
A face like a bland egg: no lips to murmur
The summer storm, wet eave, or wishing well.
No breath—perfumed Andalucía—yearning.

No human eye: affectionate fern to ring
Woodland pools the ivory bather haunted.
Lovely: hover of heaven, starlit while
The braw boar in the bracken lashed and grunted.

One hope: the sensitive orchids of all music—
To drown his grief in comfortable hair.
Fearful, his fingers sought beneath the tresses—
Screamed. And a viper of lightning hissed the air.

# OLD RIVER ROAD

### i

One party of that season. Evening journals
Whirred to their perch oblivious of doom.
The two reposed their coats. Flanked on a sofa
Sat innocent of the other. Chaffed the room

Till hands by chance encountering in cashews
(Roaming a moment from their tutor eyes)
Touched. And a current flowed. The two were dazzled:
Their hands! to play such lightning from the skies

As rocked impeccable homes to their foundation,
Loosened a promise and shook plaster down,
Baited that pack, the chaste uncharitable
Tongues till they bred contagion about town.

What matter tongues? What matter to the blinding
Mask of agony what the chorus bays?
Touched. And he doffed the satin visor: met her
Delft and undecipherable gaze

Much like the morning spangled in his lashes.
What of the brow's sereneness? Or the hair
Cool and amused, remembering crowns her fervor
Burned to the smoky gold of autumn air?

What of her gaze the gala night deciphered
Pondering mottoes of the barbarous dart?
Thanks to the ash on his lapel consulted
And the false candor of a sinking heart?

Eyes in the other's gloried like plumes tossing
That more and more sang *morituri* plain.

So gladiators in their clanking bonnet
Planting their sandals on the arrogant stain,

Eyes like coals in a great brazier glowing
Around and round the impending thousands scan,
Seizing the noon for omen! Hola, lobo!
Bloat on the rich disaster if you can.

ii

Both overfrank. In part to trip suspicion,
Part for that dragging mantle, laissez-faire,
Part for the gin, like sacred lamps attended,
They feigned embrace. A spectacle, the pair.

Anon, his tail between his legs, discretion
Deserted these, to mutter among drunks.
A spectacle of some concern to husbands,
Bumbling men unbudgeable as trunks;

Of some concern to keepers of the linen,
Bleak with the blue mondays of the past.
Their keys a-jangle: moon-resistant, May-proof.
Oh that candor were as season-fast!

Laocoön, you would have winked to see them.
Laocoön, out Lackawanna way?
Wrapped in their own bright spirals of endearment
And much aspersed by yodellers. Break of day

Found them the worse for friendly wear: a huddle
Baroque and dowdy, on a jumble of knees.
A hoyden skirt the merciful amended.
The indecent dead are howling rites like these.

Her face a sleepy flower. A child's in fever.
Once in a strange forest long ago

The birds, a shimmer of cocktail hues, came loosing
Leaves where the lost children slept below

As mist impearled the conifers. The matted
Lashes of both the tears enchanted fast.
Delicate: a rare flying thing, its lacy
Wings in the gold collodion of the past.

The tears were hard to pardon. Much-forgiving
Spouses protested water into wine.
But tears are tears. The two had each a reason:
Early morning, and the day's decline.

### iii

Brave words at first: the night of nine auroras
Rooting in curious forms of fern and wood
Chanced on a thing of earth the astonished lovers
Had scrupled to imagine if they could.

Angels beckoning Adam to the garden
Shaped with their fingers, flaming, what they meant:
Fuddled the lost lovers with indulgence
No will of theirs had ventured to invent.

They spurned the bogus bloom, cadaverous waxes,
Gathering what abounded and no more.
Stung with no iron glove the face of heaven,
Come to this pretty pass at heaven's door.

But candors flashed, admissible in marble;
Marble darkened with considerate blood;
Blood was a raging main; the embattled galleon
Toppled doubloons and javelins in the flood

As the foam scrolled: Finale. A quick curtain.
Gawky, the room and furniture trooped in.

They sagged in their embrace, strait-jackets giving;
Human heads a-loll with dingy grin.

Breath on the lip, so debonaire a spender
It left the lung no penny of its own,
Shrunk. They felt the hollow in those gaudy
Breasts that festoon the musty coops of bone.

The hollow between heartbeats; looming lobo
Hard on the heels of valor in the snow.
—What of the bright balloon, heaven's effervescence?
Trodden on fairgrounds when the wagons go

To the next town, indifferent, leaving rutted
Yesterday's joy, the fields of pleasure torn.
Where the white queens performing—swans of heaven!—
Swooned on their buoyant pole. Like twins unborn

The lovers huddle. Glittering wings that weave
Robes of the forest for our sons and daughters,
Lap them in love, who shrivel as they wait
Numbly, a spirit moving on the waters.

### iv

We are that key the fugitive finger leaves
As soaring gloria stumbles and recovers;
Chords for the Astra Khan roll kansas-black
Packing a violet fire for hidebound lovers.

Lightning: a lifeline between two and heaven
(September's not more pendulous on its stem).
Give the mad gleeman scope; the tarns of Auber
Foster a lotus moon for even them.

We knew one night the neighborhood was shaken,
Explosions underground: till two and two

The sleepers in their crazyquilt, leaves bleaching,
Mushroomed up. As broken springs would do.

Jack in his proper box. But in the pulpit?
Candor in crow or lobo, duck and drake?
An old wives' tale, remember? And what draughtsman
Caught for his rule the wrist-enchaining snake?

But even these! Her footfall shy and naked
Full on the arrogant stain as javelins rang:
A nine-days' leer to shoeclerks who live crouching,
Immaculate dentists catering to fangs.

These meant a noble fitt, but tripped on Aleph
Crooked as rails where ploughing trains collide.
And saw too much in a wrong season. Others
Suffer their trouble late, as saucers ride

Harrowing sky. The Angel of Death in heaven
(Lunatic sunrise in the dead of night)
Sows in our fallow face the ash of roses.
Dust in the eye's a charm for seeing right.

If you could come on the late train for
    The same walk
Or a hushed talk by the fireplace
    When the ash flares
As a heart could (if a heart would) to
    Recall you,
To recall all in a long
    Look, to enwrap you
As it once had when the rain streamed on the
    Fall air,
And we knew, then, it was all wrong,
    It was love lost
And a year lost of the few years we
    Account most—
But the bough blew and the cloud
    Blew and the sky fell
From its rose ledge on the wood's rim to
    The wan brook,
And the clock read to the half-dead
    A profound page
As the cloud broke and the moon spoke and the
    Door shook—

If you could come, and it meant come at the
    Steep price
We regret yet as the debt swells
    In the nighttime
And the *could come, if you could* hum in
    The skull's drum
And the limbs writhe till the bed
    Cries like a hurt thing—

If you could—ah but the moon's dead and the
    Clock's dead.
For we know now: we can give all
    But it won't do,
Not the day's length nor the black strength nor
    The blood's flush.
What we took once for a sure thing,
    For delight's right,
For the clear eve with its wild star in
    The sunset,
We would have back at the old
    Cost, at the old grief
And we beg love for the same pain—for a
    Last chance!
Then the god turns with a low
    Laugh (as the leaves hush)
But the eyes ice and there's no twice: the
    Benign gaze
Upon some woe but on ours no.
    And the leaves rush.

## DECLINE AND FALL

We had a city also. Hand in hand
Wandered happy as travellers our own land.
Murmured in turn the hearsay of each stone
Or, where a legend faltered, lived our own.
The far-seen obelisk my father set
(Pinning two roads forever where they met)
Waved us in wandering circles, turned our tread
Where once morass engulfed that passionate head.

Cornice rose in ranges, rose so high
It saw no sky, that forum, but noon sky.
Marble shone like shallows; columns too
Streamed with cool light as rocks in breakers do.

O marble many-colored as reach of thought,
Tones so recollected and so distraught.
Golden: like swimmers when the August shore
Brightens their folklore poses more and more.
Or grey with silver: moon's whirling spell
Over the breathless olives we knew well;
Ivory as shoulders there that summer-dressed
Curve to come shyly naked, then find rest
(The tresses love dishevelled leaning dazed
And grateful). Or the wayward stone that blazed
As cheeks do. Or as eyes half-lowered flare.
Violet as veins are, love knows where.
Fine coral as the shy and wild tonguetip,
Undersea coral, rich as inner lip.

There was a stone to build on!

                              Friezes ran
In strong chorales that where they closed began;
And statues: each a wrung or ringing phrase
In the soul's passionate cadence of her days.

O stone so matched and massive, worked so well,
Who could believe it when the first brick fell?
Who could imagine the unlucky word
Would darken to the worldwide sigh we heard?
How our eyes wrenched together and held fast
Each face tightening to a chalky cast
(So poor a copy of one hour before).
Who could believe the gloom, the funnelled roar
Of cornice falling, forum falling, all
Falling? Or dream it fallen? Not a wall
With eaves to route the rain. The rivers swelled
Till roads groped in lakebottom. Nothing held
Clean edge or corner. Caking, the black flood
Left every luminous room tunnels of mud.
Earth shook: the columns walked, in midair clashed,
And the steep stone exploded as it crashed.

Soon the barbarian swarmed like locusts blown
Between the flood and spasm of our stone.
Grunted to tug their huts and marble sties
Where friezes broke like foam in the blue skies.
Blue noses poked, recoiling as they found
Our young and glad-eyed statues underground;
Singing salvation, the lewd chisel pecks
At boy and girl: one mutilated sex.
All our high moments cheapened—greed and grime
Charred them in rickety stithies to quicklime.

Murderous world. That town that seemed a star
Rose in our soul. And there the ruins are.
We'll not walk there again. Who'd wish to walk
Where the rats gather and grey tourists talk?
Who'd walk there even alive? Or bid his ghost
Trail phosphor on the melancholy coast?

# POLONAISE

*"Dobranoc, kochanie . . .*
*Pamiętaj o mnie jeszcze trochę . . ."*

### 1.

The grey-green eyes, Polonia! then the bed
Throned with old trophies of a father dead.
Our star: a plane torn orange from the skies,
Szaro-zielone oczy, grey-green eyes.

Hair: bonfire gold the wind took. Blown amiss—
Half heaven lay blazing in the rain-swept kiss.
Rain taste of salt, kochanie? Cheek so cold
Under the sullen splendor, autumn gold?

Lips: in a candle's ardent trance. Or spoke
Rich in a dim significance of smoke.
Wine's lightning, lip to lip, harangued the heart:
Better the soul from body than lips part.

Sun princess, cinnamon-rose: when last we met
The panicky soldier ashen and a-sweat
Hefted his carbine, staring. Shadows close
Over a girl's defiance, cinnamon-rose.

But gardens of the breast, ecstatic still,
No passions empty and no passions fill.
No, though an eagle of Patmos warm her nest
Deep in a dole of roses, flowerbed breast.

2.

The flowering breast, Aneczka! still the dead
Vivid as poppies in the armored tread.
The east, a horde unshorn, the shaven west,
Loll in the half-track hooting, flowery breast.

Sun princess, cinnamon-rose: across your cheek
Mark of the darkness speaking when you speak?
Our willow, lovelock in the Vistula, knows
Dark of the moon becomes you, cinnamon-rose.

Hair, ember gold. Pan's tendril at the ear
Dusky with lovesongs of the darkening year.
Trains blunt as thunder, eye almighty, rolled
Over the gala shoulder, autumn gold.

Lips: in a candle's ardent trance. Or wine
Breathing Slavonian starlight in the pine.
At Biskupin—the enchanted cabins—start
Tales of the parted lips, the lips apart.

The grey-green eyes, rain-driven, fade afar.
What journey's end for children of the star?
Courage! He sings—great father—from the skies
Of szaro-zielone ever, grey-green eyes.

NOTE: The Polish phrase of line 4, translated by the words
that follow it, is pronounced rather like *sháh-doe zhe-láwn-
eh áwe-chee*. Biskupin is an ancient lake settlement in west-
ern Poland—one can still see remains of the primitive huts
in the marsh.

# II

*αἱ δὲ τεαὶ ζώουσιν ἀηδόνες*

## THE EVERGREEN

a.

*Under this stone, what lies?*
    A little boy's thistledown body.
*How, on so light a child*
    *Gravel hefted and hurled?*
Light? As a flower entwined
    In our shining arms. Heavy
Laid in this scale—it set
    Wailing the chains of the world.

## b.

*What did you say?* We said:
    Bedtime, dear, forever.
Time to put out the light.
    Time for the eyes to close.
*What did he do?* He lay
    In a crazyquilt of fever.
His hands were already like grasses.
    His cheek already a rose.

## C.

*How was that year?* His voice.
   Over sun on the rug, slow-turning,
Hung like a seabird lost the
   Lorn and bodiless cry.
Haunting the house. *And then?*
   I remember then. One morning
Silence like knives in the ear.
   A bird gone over the sea.

### d.

*What of his eyes?* Dark glow
    Furling the world's great surface.
Bubbles among tree lights;
    Bubbles of ferny dew.
*And his kiss?* On our cheek at evening
    Vintage: a fine bursting.
*This, and never dreamed his*
    *Span was a bubble too?*

e.

Little head, little head,
    Frail in the air, gold aster—
Why did the great king stoop
    And smoothe those ringlets down?
*For a tinsel party-hat?*
    *It was Christmas then, remember?*
I remember grown men wept
    And couldn't lift that crown.

f.

*Mother, these tears and tears?*
    The better to see you, darling.
*Mother, your golden glasses—*
    Have a sorry fault,
Being made for things, dear,
    Mostly: carts and marbles.
Mothers wear, for children,
    Better the stinging salt.

## g.

*What you remember most—?*
Is a way of death with fingers.
How they are cast in tallow
—Lover!—webbed as one.
*Where was he going, with webs?*
*A flying child? or a swimming?*
He knew, where he went,
One way back to the sun.

### h.

"Tesoro!" implored the maid.
    "Treasure!" the tall signora.
*Under a distant heaven*
    *What struck the famous tower?*
Faults in the earth despairing.
    Worlds away, an orchard
Offered violets early.
    And we returned a flower.

### i.

*Where does he lie?* Hill-high
    In a vision of rolling river.
Where the dogwood curls in April
    And June is a dream of Greece.
Like a Christmas scene on china,
    Snow and the stubborn myrtle.
*Those flakes from feathery heaven—?*
    Deepen all in peace.

## j.

*Where does he rest, again?*
    In a vision of rolling river.
*What does he know of river?*
    What do we know of sea?
*Comfort?—when tomorrow's*
    *Cheek by jowl with never?*
Never . . . in whose garden
    Bloomed the used-to-be.

## k.

*Under the snow, what lies?*
    Treasure the hemlock covers—
Skysail of frost, and riding in
    Starlight keen and steep.
*But the boy below?* What's here is
    Gear in a sea-chest only.
Stowed for a season, then
    Pleasure-bound on the deep.

# III

*Venídom es deliçio    de tierras d'allén mar*

# PARALLAX AT DJEBEL-MUTA

He strolled the desert cliff; tumultuous sunset
Drove a long shadow, phantom, over sands,
Honeycombed long ago—a thunder of granite
Teeters, pitching him down. Numb knees and hands

Gather beneath him; now he droops and rolls
Like a floored boxer his enormous head.
Ten feet above, a jagged edge of sky.
He had a flashlight; gropes, topples instead

Something that rocks like pottery; then the cool
Grooves of chromium fumbled-on in gloom.
Shadows—a black on sepia danse macabre—
Rage in a forty-century-old tomb.

Under an inch of dust, some rags and bone,
Rubble of royalty. The trained eye reads
Skulls of a boy and girl: his lank with fracture,
Hers in a constellation of blue beads.

Cinnamon, cassia, clove, mysterious such
Run from the tippy skull like hourglass sand:
The girl's hair caught close for windy riding,
A ruined cheek lagoons of lotus tanned,

And a whole shoulder by the broken bone
Nearly intact. El Greco lean. Stroked
By fingers shy as a new lover's it
Absently fell apart like ashes poked.

See the man hunched there? See his bleeding knee
Jostle the thirsty bone that, lacquered, dulls
Immediately like blotters? See him breathe
A stuff once sweeter, sounder than all bells?

✧

Yes and the'll be a day when waters weeping
The tale of time sing fountains in the park,
The hourglass bud with butterflies and iris,
And dials doff old hawsers of the dark.

✧

Spring on the desert cliff: a wonder of sunrise
Fair on the chariot sporting Re, his disk
And halo of hooded snakes. Imported horses,
Plumes of flamingo and eye rolling, risk

A four-spoke bumping bronze wheel on the limestone
Lip of the gorge; the riders shout and lean:
She smiling, Nile-green eyes steady, golden
Throat and one shoulder bare. Do you think a queen?

Well his queen. Green pleats belted round his middle,
Shoulders armorial bronze, rein-sailing hand,
With falcon eyes half-shadowed on her, laughing,
Like skiers down and over the dazzling sand

Balancing paired—as for a season flesh
Glories, adoring any dare of soul.
Wide-circling, they rein in: sinew-corded
Burgeoning pillars by a ferny pool

Under two touselled palms: knotted sandals
Squeal in the padded sand; the lovers' lips
Explore at ease in their lost language, spelt with
Hawks looking hard at you, baboons and ships,

Bee, bittern, king of beasts, the crescent moon—
Flesh and blood alphabet. (Their flesh and blood,
So rich a drift on thornstock of the bone!)
—Even as they kiss, the ghost appeared, midflood

*36 ·*

In sunlight, as in mingle of moonlight once
He came inspecting with archaic stare.
A rickety skeleton, horn-circled eyes,
Ore in his teeth, a wide skull without hair;

Left arm leathered to a prank of time;
Right, dry splinters, poking a chrome rod;
Before him buttons floating in air pit-patter
Castanets on his breastbone with each nod.

A breath of air his ruin. Teasing, they
Wheedle him near. Until lips radiant still
Panic the ghost. They, whistling their wild horses,
Sprang and like golden eagles took the hill.

## *ETRUSCAN TOMB*

Tarchna dreams by the distant ocean—
Nobody knows how long a dream.
Sorts of lore
Old when the testy cardinal, blazing,
Ripped his sword from the heinous beam;
Old before:
Look, strange hordes on the bristling shore.
What a humus of tombs! and the ghosts and tokens
Storm like gulls at the furrowing team.

Time out of mind a ledge in a meadow
Nobody saw as heft of hands,
Rainy-grey,
Passed with a glance by the steely Romans
Frowning bigger and better plans—
Now, today,
Look, we have pried stone doors away!
What a burst of birds and frolic of dolphins
Swirling the air like banners and bands!

How they were drunk with hope, these children!
Nobody told them life was dour.
Gloomy tombs?
What, when tombs were salons for living!
Nothing had ended, that was sure.
Laurel blooms,
Look, in the bright, bird-flirting rooms.
What a chuckle of jugs, what crooning copper!
Flowers festooning the furniture!

And treasure catching the breath! in mines why
Nobody struck such eager wealth.
Oh no glow
Of morose ruby, viperous emerald
Here: here's candor and flush of health.
On this stone,
Look! what an outdoor field-fest thrown!
What a bright lense catching the dancers' passion,
Brow's abandon and barefoot stealth.

Horsemen flash on the sundrunk meadow—
Nobody drank so mad a sun,
Shoulders bold.
Eyes in rainbow of golden lashes
Laugh as the high-knee horses run.
Slick as coal,
Look! and the skyblue feyfoot foal!
What a hover of hooves like rippling fingers,
Manes that tangle and thunderous fun.

So friskily ferned and folked an ocean
Nobody sour of spirit knows.
Radiant haze
On the prism cliff and the waves that plop with
Lollop of dolphin springy as bows.
Bathers gaze,
Look, where the innocent fishline strays.
What a plunge from the reef as seabirds scatter!
Bodies simple as flowers unclose.

Though their tongue is a wild conundrum,
Nobody had such lucid hands:
Soothe or hoot,
Confer gently with troubled horses,
Reassure like a loving glance,
Cuddle fruit,
Look, and dazzle the twosome flute!
What a blur of birds! and the wingtip fingers!
Swallowy palms floating over the dance.

That dance! hips like a whisk of fingers;
Nobody had such flings of fun,
Flair as there!
No girl swung on a flank of satin,
None in a shiver of sequin spun
As these wear,
Look! pure limbs and halo of hair.
What a splendor of flesh! as if bones were breathing
Slender a fire as the virgin dawn.

Man's tomb—for the rest what greensick symbols.
Nobody else had lip so live,
Eye so fired.
Others mutter their maybes, pleading
Peacock, phoenix, and yew survive.
Tarchna choired
Look! what the soul itself desired.
What a mumble of skulls and dust from others.
All she sang was *Alive oh alive.*

Tarchna's death is a dive in sunlight.
Nobody knows how deep a dive—
See that sea!
Flung like sun in a seethe of rainbows
Drenched and laughing the dead arise!
Just to be
Look! in so wild bright brash a sea!
What a thunder of surf! and the great locks tossing.
Still she sang *Oh alive and alive.*

Tarchna's dark: in the bronzing twilight
Nobody treks the haunted run.
Broken loam
Scuffing the musk of age and autumn.
Westward, ah the effulgent zone.
Far below
Look! how the carmine harbors glow!
What a thrilling of red like brilliant music,
Like eyelids fast on a rapture of sun.

# ROMAN LETTER

S.D.A.C.

*inventas aut qui vitam excoluere per artis
quique sui memores alios fecere merendo*

What stormy barometers of emotion blown,
Upheaval in heaven, spells of moon and thunder
Over pediments piled to stupefy barbarians!
*Odi et amo*—girls of the region reaped a
Murderous wind: Rome's ornery as mortality.

Colossal oddments like a hollywood midden,
Lonely location of old superfilms.
How many a neighborhood in double exposure,
Epoch on epoch overthrust, outcropping;
Centuries telescoped like famous trains.

Look at the forum like old molars patched,
Clamps a-grapple and the bogus brick.
Deride if you will—but scuffing the chariot ruts
Of the Sacred Way, such panic of remembrance,
Such brunt of fact, delirium of old triumph
Thuds on the nape of your neck that reason reels.

Except for languor of the world's pretension,
The exhilarance of death and outer space,
Except for the platitudes in aquarelle,
Who'd love the stones of Rome—such brutal spoor
Tracking the verdigris and chalcedony?
The skull of the Colosseum, eaten clean,
(My charming American Daisy, Dublin Maud)
Eroded as old bone, dead as the moon—
What's the right tribute but the eye's aversion?

Remember the Lateran's gilded pugilist,
Thorax swollen like cobra's, cobra head,
Caligula's petted bullyboy?—there's your token.
Where else has propaganda such a pedigree?

It's hard to remember holiness was here
(Though never at home: was here with every horror
Of iron blurting red, of blood-soaked leather)
And left strange traces: a house of God, and aping
Some deified Julian's pool, some de luxe terminal?—
Bragging it's pure: no tourist with bare shoulders;
Bragging boisterously its big physique.

Sanctity's in the cellar yet. Those mines of
Silence and wild conundrum catch the breath.
Saints play at find-the-tomb: all's fabulous
The chisel chinks on here. Reach and rub wonder.

Shaken, reascend to the marble barns—
It's hard to forgive this temple! Best forget,
For Sant' Agnese, San Clemente, Quattro
Coronati, San Prassede's zodiac roof—
All reliquaries, a rapt jeweler's dream:
With God's great eye in jade, his hurricane hair,
His wrestlers and his virgins fierce as trees
Striving and staring where? Beyond. Their passion
Tugs at the world's inertia till it soars.

In Rome, encourage your eye to panorama,
Look far and wide; be chary of close looks
Where highfalutin pilasters weave, performing
St. Vitus' rites. (Cambodia's fevered stone

Is haunted so.) Never mind. We soon accept
As we accept the family bats in belfries,
The taints of a loved face. Come to require them
And wouldn't be without.

                    The face of Rome:
Imperial and autumnal, her remote
Blue eyes half-drowsed with multifarious loves,
Lips stirred voluptuously, the corners still
Triste with atrocities of long ago.
No queen perhaps—an actress all distraction
To men. A face to be milled in mellow gold.

Her color's gold. The color of cut melon
Gives succulence to any lean perspective.
Rome's all air and distance. Where is space
Such an impresario as here? So musical?
With water fluting from shells or plashing its palms
On rataplan troughs or timpani of water;
With air (from high Frascati or the sea's
Black-lava shore Tyrrhenian bathers hail)
A glossy talker in oriels of the laurel
Or tolling the tragic attitude of pines.

Pause on the brink of the Spanish Steps at evening
When the twilight-blooming youth, pale castaways,
Wash to that far-seen crag from every land,
And the schoolgirls swirl in their dirndls to sit like lotus;
Or stray on the Pincio redolent of the great
Great dead: look west to the Tiber and Monte Mario,
Where three domes in a row increase and hover
Like balls in a conjurer's palm.

An olio too mauve for candor of beauty,
Too flushed and mournful-eyed, with a trace of tremolo,

Yet here we'd live, and not for the saffron pergolas,
The picnic under the tomb in the Appian meadow—
But for prodigies and a cue or two, the pressure
Of many an atmosphere—all that impregnates
The pine by Egeria's water, the embosoming air.

# FLORENCE

FOR SALLY AND ROBERT

The yellow river and the violet hills
Henry James embossed in permanent-black
Jollied a flagging fellow to exuberance.
He saw the angel of Florence: cozy-gold.

This arrogant beauty soothe, who's least a flatterer?
Her suavity silk-on-steel; her ease ironic,
Queen of the pageant fox and panther lead.

On Bellosguardo's scarp (the intoning ghost
Our conscience and our quest; his cypresses
Leathery grenadiers for the lost causes)
Clamber the cobbled ramps in clarion air
To a gravel belvedere breezy and cedary
Lavishing:

       Florence mortised in her hills,
Oxide-rose, a glory of quartz sunning.

Misnomer of blossomy nods, stern fleur-de-lys,
Igneous stone's your heritage and mood.

Over all, the ebullient dome, great brazen hub
Of the derelict circus-wheel of faith parading.
Michelangelo, off for Rome, raged at that cupola,
Eyelids hooding gruff energies of love:
"Excel her I cannot. Copy her—damned if I will!"

There's Florence to the core: those canyon spaces
Dry as adobe air, a sunset flush
Of memory burning where the glamorous name
Toppled, the weapon wedged in his skull, blonde hair

Sopped like a diver's: passionate Sandro spun
As panic rent the veil of the Mass; as blood
Wrote fast on the floor; Lorenzo behind portals
Paced tiger-thighed in rioting partisans,
Tear-spangled face a comet of imprecation.

Or the cotes of watery gold where Dante hefted
His sledge till the marble stung like spray!

                        Above,
How Giotto's mother-of-pearl recorder glories
Over tubas of cloud, over jubilant woodwind blue!

But listen: testy antiphons come wrangling
From the Palazzo Vecchio, haggard shawm.
Here's varmint-eyed, hard-bit, surly Firenze,
The snarl in the name, no name of blossoms now:
The hanged man's booted somersault from merlons;
Gullet stairs stilettoed bodies bump.

Duck with a sheepish cocktail under its turbulence,
Tourist in sporty shorts. The immense contempt
Of a truncheon torn from thorn, of fangy battlements,
Of a rusty-gold old hauberk-harsh façade
Panics your chattering camera to far corners,
Looms like an old bogy's matterhorn.
Compose its face to serene avatars,
Shrink it to atavism—not a flicker
From the craggy brows that rake Siena still
Through mountainous indigos of execration.

So to the river: yellow after showers
In quercine purlieus of the Casentine
Busy their taupe melodeons, clarabella.

Then Tuscan silt yaws cargoed to the sea.

She's a glum trawler then. But other mornings
Ply the sweet-minded mirrors.

                        Under the sunset
Her loitering dreamers, hunched toward Pisa, know
Dire aurum like the Arbia's: heinous red
You sniff in the wind still. What passion hangs
Over the ruined bridges! Underwater
The smoky palms of divers, webbed with mud,
Probe in lunging murk for the lost features.

Streets we essayed at every hour: those piquancies
Are graven deep in the brain—the nostril's tingle
At pine-shavings on pavements when the rain
Purpled the somber gorge of Vigna Nuova;
Or flower-banks under the granite mien, a sweetness
Coddled and mocked by dubious ambience:
Boisterous savor of hot herbs from kitchens;
Halls ether-sweet with desuetude; the celery
Reek in lichenous archways, iron-railed
Against such pungency: rankness of time,
Of human life and human love—its mouldering
Packed in the common halidoms we plod.

It's Rome for all cajolery. This Florence
You find in your own heart, if anywhere,
Prizers of wild acridity, sunset-crimson
Rancor of peach too near the rusty pit,
Or thralls of a northern calm, camellia-white
Of swimmers dripping from numb monochrome.

Surely no pendulous angel: cozy-gold.

O candor-of-almond cheek, cool lashes' raillery
Under the lancers' eave one drenching day,
Serene in the great hotel's flurry of foreigners,
Or niched from pitiless snow in San Frediano's
Grot of a door, by the bleak Bar's fluorescence,
Your hair a sowing of stars, oblivious lady—

From over time and the sea my gift, carissima.
Bear it with bantering palm: rough everlastings,
Thistles purple as stelliferous night.

# REFLECTIONS IN VENICE

Except for the dowdy splash in back canals,
The lettuce and the lemon bold as brass,
All of that uppity ruckus on the radiant
Bayous dreaming of Byzantium yet,
Who'd ever assent to Venice? Who'd believe?

Men fancy pueblos so in the grand affair
Of a calliope sunset, see them plain
Through thirst over the witty sand's delirium.
Men have whimsies—but indulge them in marble?
Throw a bold roof on hallucination?
"Venice unseats the reason." Rather say
Reason became a delicate madman, chortled
Over preposterous blueprints. And approved them.
The daily bread's absurdity. What can never
Exist (for all of the bees in reason's bonnet)
You stub your toe on. The best leather scuffs.

Because the incredible's hourly and of course,
What takes the breath is wonder of banality:
The gondolier's shovelling shoulder, quirky wrist
(His long stroke like a billow tripped on shale)
Sculling not lovers but a bathtub, rags,
Mattresses, cabbage, or a coop with cacklers;
While over his sousing route one traffic light,
Alice's tabby—look!—appearing, disapp—

A straight line here?—anathema! Sobersided
Cities behave like waffles. Venice no.
Her gold palazzi ripple like theater curtains
When a door opens offstage on reality.
That Venice in the water, upside-down,
Is nearly as sound, as practical to live in.

Her skin: a great sea-creature hauled ashore,
Rind, hackle, hide and dewlap beached and fading
Under that glare from splendor of the depths
To grey of shale and pebble, of kelp sunning.

Watch how the walkers bob like kangaroo
Over the little bridges (pretty rickrack:
Wickets for the ancient sea disporting).
Streets are a crinkum-crankum, lithographed
Gameboard of Advance Three or Back to Start,
Left in a night of rain to bleach and frizzle.

What's for a prize? Ca' d'Oro: faded seine,
Her grey and coral plaited to catch time.
Opposite, in the fishmart, brooms of bracken
Scuffle the onion, orange-paper, sage.

What's for a prize? San Marco, malapert
To Parthenon-doting eyes: extravagant baggage!

A Cretan dancer on back somersault
Arching breast-up on ivory heel and finger.

At sunset, like a Valentine afire
That nick of time before it sags and blackens.

Tawny and sweet within, dark honeycomb
Of buckwheat shuffled with bright combs of clover.

Above, the dome's old glow—an artist's bowl
Where grime of gold was puddled till it crusted,
Left in a cupboard under cellar stairs
—A cat's eye in a jungle!—among cobwebs.

Hers is a floor, no, not to walk—to wade:
Lurching like sandbars under surf. Our weight
Thrills in the pitch and drag of seafloors drained,
The flora charmed, the osprey flat as fossils.

And the great souls that people the dark mountain!
Massing in fabulous funnies, fey charade.

Their gestures few as semaphores know poses.

Woe's a contusion, joy a vivid gash
On faces scored like boxers': chuck-full
Of rough conviction, nuggets in a gunny sack.

Where these parade, in stalagmite for toga,
The stone's alive: four-footed homes, pagodas
Shamble on pillar shank like headless pets.
All's neighborly: the houses men step out of
Crouch at their heel and sit there till commanded,
Handy as stools. The fishermen ease rumps
Into the cockleshells they're broader than.
All as it should be. These were made for mortals.

As mortals were for God. Why should great spirits
Fuss and truckle to pernickety blubber?
They've better things to con than right anatomy—
Eyes spellbound on the languorous green prince
Draped zigzag on his crisscross; on the angels
Gawky as new-hatched eagles from the shell;
On the great father's caving face of doom,
Beard like a snowslide in the Pyrenees.

Leaving the trance of northern night, go blinking
Into a blizzard of pigeons. Puzzle on it:

Venice, a shopworn rainbow. Maybe. But
In time's kaleidoscope what spunkier sparkle
As the great kingdoms pyramid and slip?
If man must have a single den, be denizen,
Venice would do. As well as Waffleopolis,
Suburbia's forty winks, or Little Wotting.

She'll set the wits a-tintinnabulating!

Restorative music in our time. And sovereign
For many a subtle canker. If it's granted
Our grief is of the heart or of the reason,
Settle in Venice, traveller—lose both.

# CATULLUS

*Desideratoque acquiescimus lecto*

At Sirmio on Garda
Flaunts the enchanting castle.
Their trunks rococo as harps, blonde
Olives fondle a theme.

Through Garda's blue siesta
It's love in the wind. The Roman
Stone resounds it: Love. The
Tendril affirming the rune.

Off Sirmio, blue swells are
Belling a shoalway of gold. These
Green like furious fern. Two
Colors seething in one.

Garda: sea-race and rock. Was
Water so stalwart ever?
Marble ever so fluent? Or
Time so enduring a shore?

# FUORI STAGIONE

*Caro m'è il sonno, e più
l'esser di sasso . . .*

In ivory, at Verona
The Scaliger ride high.
Fervently *he* companioned
Old corpses in the sky.

Venice: lugubrious wherries
Shiver the weird lagoon.
Pale on the pitching wharf, crews
Ululate the moon.

Santa Croce, tolling floor.
His memorial toe
Tracing a shawled effigy
Wormed itself below.

Ravenna then, her dogged
Vaults' auriferous gloom.
Our tardy suitor
Hugged Placidia's tomb.

And Rome: the protochristians'
Cindery honeycomb.
He in the marvellous dark came
Thunderstruck home.

# A FRIEZE OF CUPIDS

*Qui su l'arida schiena*
*Del formidabil monte*
*Sterminator Vesevo . . .*

Pompeii: the seedy vendors
Ruffle and palm their books
Under the tourists'
Stirred or averted looks.

One gathers men loved women
Millenniums ago.
How, and how much? The tourists
Pay furtively to know.

Visions mauve and tender.
Scenes queasily sad:
The grey grit laid forever
Whatever bloom they had.

Lava composed their spirit.
Withered the wing of pride.
The mountain lapped these lovers
In a long side-by-side.

Our incest-ridden mumbler
Heard the great mother call—
His sick effusion dooming
The children one and all.

# IV

*Que ni poso en ramo verde,—ni en prado que tenga flor;*
*que si el agua hallo clara,—turbia la bebía yo . . .*

## ORIGINATED IN A CHORUS
## OF SATYRS

Had eager Eve for whose sweet will we languish,
Had Adam culled the garden as he should,
What of the great tale then: stone torso of anguish
Lost for the soft samoas of the wood?
Which of the three hurled *mawkish* at the florid
Dead-end of time? God's proxy manned to act?
Eve pondering palm on thigh? The Andean forehead
Blazing in clouds and lightning: *false to fact?*

Whose notion to explode the halcyon deadlock,
Dunging the garden with felicitous sin?
Harrow the native clay? Go clean to bedrock?
Which of the three hailed scathing vision in
When the eighth day made history?

                              Pity and dread
Blazon like haloes the great blinded head.

# ANCIENT OF DAYS

Spellbound as lunar buttes, the terrible past
Because it lies before me chills the bone.
In Knossos at high noon I mooned, dreamfast
On girls cartwheeling in sunflowers over the stone,
Schist or selenite. Or heard of worse:
Tar cocoons in earth the effendis sight
And syphoning in hot wax, tease back to birth
Ecce-homo's of lip-withering night.

Unless the opposable thumb (with crown and crozier:
Not pottering now in fields of Pleistocene)
Prove to our joy the pearly world's disposer
And not time's by-blow, as sucked craniums mean:—
Souls' saturnalia then! the moon's great gong
Enthralling the fairy pintos of the dawn!

Sweeten the moody world, Milesian waters,
Sparkle on Ur, on Lagash where it lies;
Drenching in dew the fertile crescent, scatter
The rosegold rumps babooning in the skies.
Flow to the squatting mother, nipples rigid,
Pupils of milkglass from the idiot sun,
Nursing her private Nile—over the turgid
Cats of the sand let freshets bubble and run

Rafting the first man ever to stand upright,
Ever through aqueous humor view the world,
Even its pyramids!—who (dared their true height)
Eyed the wide shadow on dominions hurled,
Bestriding his own: huffed gilas when he spoke
Ruptured like puffballs in irascible smoke.

## AFFAIR AT THE FORK

The gods leaned forward at his bursting forth
Thick-booted out of Corinth, hating the business,
Hellbent for anywhere else. Rampaging north
(His face an icon of dust from the dim isthmus)
He clashed with foreigners where ruts contorted,
Glorying, "Room for the king of Corinth's son!"
High in the cart, an apparition snorted
And ground the hub on his leg—the sensitive one.

Damnation! Blind with pain, his temples pealing,
He wrestled the gauntface down, brow stunning brow,
Rolled savage among slaves, till passion cooling
Crooned for him tunes of decent headway now.
The gods sank back enchanted: flattering bell!
When had the fractious planet run so well?

# CALLIOPE TO CLIO

μῆνιν ἄειδε, θεά, Πηληιάδεω ᾿Αχιλῆος
οὐλομένην, ἣ μυρί᾿ ᾿Αχαιοῖς ἄλγε᾿ ἔθηκε

The red wrath of Achilles—cope with that,
Muse, if you dare. Look doting on disaster:
Heroes dumped arsy-versy in hades' grot,
Lurid as lava pattering faster faster.
Flesh given to dogs—what bloomed in a queen's eye
Angry elastic snaggled in the fang;
And what the soaked crows spatter as they fly;
All this. Last, how the oxhorn lamina rang

As the lounging god (in profile to display
Better the measured nose, serene lip curling),
Called nonchalantly his targets, and let fly
With whinny of pleasure arrows cool as sterling.
That statue of him, though broken: the fine eye
Flicks unconcerned—why not?—the unnerving sky.

# AGAMEMNON BEFORE TROY

*Er will blos zeigen, wie es
eigentlich gewesen*—RANKE

A-traipsin' from a shindig, I unsaddles—
Three floozies an' a blatherin' buckaroo
Wangled the whole caboodle, and skedaddles.
You in cahoots with thet shebang, skidoo!—
Seein' if yer the critters I suspicion,
You varmints ain't a-goin' to hotfoot far.
Sartin galoots is sp'ilin' fer conniptions—
Wal, they's a posse hustlin' here an' thar

Fixin' to put the kibosh on shenanigans
By landin' scalawags in the calaboose.
Hornswoggled! sich palaver with bamboozlin'
Coyotes gits my dander up! Vamoose
Totin' spondulicks an' the cutie too!
They're itchin' fer a whangdang howdy-do!

# ISHTAR

Two ordinary people, nextdoor neighbors—
Surely nothing for legend in these two:
He swishing in mint (his only labors)
Whirring matched irons over clover and dew.
And she for parties: the gold lighter poises
Shy in her fingers, an assyrian bird.
A downward smile, gilt sandals flexing. Voices
Curl in a pillowy corner, half unheard.

That night, the bedlamp fitful in her room;
Panes staring black and anxious. A race
Of lightning (thunder held, amassing doom)
Quivered long drenching seconds on each face.

Sweet firebird, fly away; fade, golden shoe.
Wait long and long, bright irons, for the dew.

## *THE LADY*

Had she an inch of cloth for every kiss
The lady were demurest among nuns,
Who wears alone the holy moon for dress,
Earthy creations of the day undone.
Her sole floats marble warm, endears the dark,
Raising a chapel in the ivory night.
Stars offer silk and sequin, but the stars
Move dubious, misdoubting white on white.

Who's to be sure but God with second glance
First knew his mind as April?—*these shall live.*
What neither Grecian eave nor plumes of France
Nor Hungary's tomb, the lady won: survive.
As baubles know their office, thrones their role,
The lady shows of what the soul is soul.

# A PRETTY DEVICE OF
# THE FATHERS

A dagger (whose bone haft the iceberg locks)
Prime diamond in the nights of polar cold:
Sharpened by shamans haloed in white fox,
Their faces bland (obols of scythian gold)—
Butt fused in ice: the uncanny tool upstanding
Whetted so fine it sang in the least wind,
A glamor the grey lopers took to haunting,
Each eye a prickle of fire: wolves winter-thinned

Pad furry-eyed, tongues hankering for that bangle
(Bobbing like censers to the illustrious vault):
One runs a tongue along the edge: a tingle
Teases him, warm and sticky, thrilling of salt.
Delirious attar of life! The ecstatic glare
Glues them in furry carnage, sweet fangs bare.

## NATIONE NON MORIBUS

### (1265-1321)

   ... shrug off the world (as churning boys
     leather head tucked, shake tacklers and reel free)
     forgetting, just like that, the ingenious toys,
red hearts and yellow hair, the unstable quay,
     that tedium and Te Deum of our days,
     and with a mind clean as amnesia see:
the wanderer's double world, where intermaze
     (gold comb in gypsy hair) the event and vision:
     the Roman mouth its dark as copper phrase
long under dust, imperious with decision;
     woods hoarse and murky as unloading of coal,
     bitch-eyed libido the light air's derision—
       then, from the deck of planets as they roll
       to breathe that air! And breathless ... at the Pole ...

# V

*Steekt geen afval in de asbakjes, dank U.*

# *THE MIRROR*

High holiday: the castle lank with banners
Swam like pagodas streamered undersea.
In gaudy gloom, rough honeycomb the casement;
Chink and rathole flash orfèvrerie.
By barbican or moat, in bramble shambling
The zany with his glittery smithereen,
Cutting the palm that fondles it—but catching
Cerise, cerulean, amber, grecian-green.

A hulker in the pitiless briar, a chuckler
Scuffing irascible honeybees of light.
The mirror shoots and cools. A briny iris
—Wandering wildfire of the outer night—
Cozily winks: a porcupine, that castle,
Spiny with fires that ravish and derange.
Lips flitter to the moon a rainbow spittle.
Cloudy as turning worlds the great eyes change:

Green with the misty liturgy, pale satin;
Roan where hairy forearms bang the board;
Quince with the leman fingers stealing thighward;
Gold where the black dwarf hunches—lo the lord!
Sheet-lightning eye, beard caracul as thunder,
Palms flickering dispensation, flaring wide
From twin tornado of purple sleeves; enthroned like
Genii of weather on the great divide.

The lord of rule and misrule, of the revels:
Outrager of fable in the sacred wood.
His image storms the oriels like voltage,
A maelstrom in the critter's pool of blood.

Who heard the one cry splintered among starlight?
Saw the moon-creature slump forevermore?
Not the fiesta-folk, whose dapper ceiling
Mirrors the ceiling mirrored in the floor.

When currents stir, and the blond soul of candles
Flee without giving ground, as dancers go,
When gusts in the wild arras plague the hunter,
His brow set deadly on the golden doe—
Only the weather eye avails up-current,
Sails by a ringlet drenched, a foundering light,
Home to that broken oak, to timbers giving
Under the weight of silence and the night.

# THE NECROMANCERS

## I

Clowns in a garish air. On panicky pedals
Managing monocycles for dear life.
And the heart pumps a ruby hoop—Fortuna's.
The princess flings our halo, knife by knife.

## II

Tally the take in that affair with glory.
How I lay gaudy on the barbarous shore
Face burrowing in a patch of fern, blood stirring
Gamy as wines remembering summer stir.
No vein of all this flesh but leapt with memory:
Such splendor on lip and finger and the rest
As noon on a great range of sea, as heaven's
Moody amour, confusing east and west.

In grottos hung with cork and cordage bobbling
On halcyons where the lascar and his shade
Lay fecund in feluccas, hearts atumble
Made love a plague of angels, raving, unmade.

Deep comas of the sun! My loafing shoulder
Ached for the sweetness pillared on your palm.
Ear to the ground heard dusky tambours: *coming.*
A crackle of skirt, sails bantering with calm.
The weight of sweetness then! I saw it settle
(Curled on a whirling skirt) in my dark dream.
And jubilant: *honey and sun, the blood!* Music
Demurred from the warm dark: *inhuman stream*!

A voice from long ago. And the warm darkness
Shuddered how often on the barbarous shore

Since two defied, palms conjuring, a bayou
The bitterns boom adieu, and guard no more.

The wheel that fractured light has come full-circle.
Leans with the poky spoke dust deepens on.
Ours sang and singing died. But all one summer
Who knew for sure that wonder from the sun?

### III

Clowns in a garish air. On panicky pedals
Managing monocycles for dear life.
And the heart pumps a ruby hoop—Fortuna's.
The princess flings our halo, knife by knife.

In love with shadows all our days,
Creepers shunning dark and bright:
The dutiful, who troop to gaze
On friendship's long-exhausted rite;
To fob and shuffle palm to palm
Coppers of accustomed thought:
Decades have tested all we say;
And we lope roguish, as they taught.

Beneath the mistletoe will drift
Kisses the flat "punch" half warms.
Wan mirage of kisses. No
Likelihood of thunderstorms.
Compilers would look far to find
Milder perversities of lust.
There is no ruby in this ash:
Kisses that half stir the dust.

White shoulders we would press today—
Time is a great page torn between!
We nibble polite watercress
Fresher than memory, more green
Than Junes which gloated-over here
Would blast the many-eyebrowed room,
Alarming almost to its feet
The tableau stable as a tomb.

From where the soul with level look
Is hinting its contempt too well,
We flee—who cannot be alone—
Like bats poured panicky from hell.

From where the eye we dare not meet
Burns ruby in immortal bronze,
We break and run like giggling kids—
Ecstatic if a portal clangs.

Is there no lightning in the land
To show us, bitter black and white,
The car, the cottage, and the dune,
The hound a-howling all that night,
And where the imprudent, hand in hand,
Sway naked in immortal surf?
What vision haunts the summer land?
What wound is closing in the turf?

Shrimp on little picks impaled
Lie naked to the decent eye,
Grey frost their bed. Our fingers lift,
Insert them goggling, and put by—
Quashing a thunder in the soul
That rages to make all things right:
In love with shadows all our days,
Creepers shunning dark and bright.

# THE CAVEMAN ON THE TRAIN

When first the apprizing eye and tongue that muttered
(Banished from Eden's air? Or pride of apes?)
Sat clinking flint on flint, and as they shattered
Snatched with a grin what fell in craftier shapes,
The law was move or die. Lively from tigers;
Dainty on deer. As weather called the tune.
Oxen, we learned, would bear us. So would rivers.
And that was science. On the whole a boon.

What caveman on a round rock dumped a-grunting
Rubbed at a rueful hip, brow darkening *why?*
Or gaped at boulders over gravel shifting
Until—a splendor of wheel-thought like sunrise!
No wonder: such example in a heaven
Revving immaculate gears, and at his feet
The planet on her axle greased and even.
Put any wheel to earth, and two wheels meet.

Athens cut ruts of marble; ivory courses
Caromed Apollo's car of talkative gold.
And Donne saw wagon-ways. The horsepower: horses.
Over the flats of Kansas sail-cars rolled.
First planks on querulous ground, then treads of metal,
Steel set edgewise, over stone for ties.
A mountain? Sawtooth rail or crank-and-cable
Till iron took serene the incredulous rise.

Compleat with a nifty moniker, *Puffing Billy,*
*Best Friend of Charleston, Wabash Cannonball,*
*Cycloped* (horse on treadmill trudging), dapper
Black and gold of Byzantium, *Sans Pareil*

Flew in the face of time and testy weather,
Enemies both, the lurid brakemen know.
(By stoves where sand is baking crisp, they gather
Trading the tall tales of high-striding snow.)

The lone prairie, the twilight grey as steel,
The vanishing freight—oh see the lonely road
Our fathers wandered, stumbling on the wheel
—Daydreamers all, and the long row unhoed—
Sky-hankering men, their reverence still alive
Some years ago: with burning glass and sun
George Stevenson in 1825
Snatched fire for *Locomotion No. 1.*

Ten miles an hour, "immoderate" twelve. Today
*Slow Down to Ninety,* warns the black ravine.

He will go far, the caveman, this-a-way.

By grand indifference to the red and green.

# VI

*¡Quién hubiese tal ventura—sobre*
*las aguas de mar . . . !*

# ON THE BANKS OF THE DUERO

[Antonio Machado, *A Orillas del Duero*]

*Mediaba el mes de julio. Era un hermoso día.*
*Yo, solo, por las quiebras del pedregal subía . . .*

We were halfway through July. Handsome afternoon!
All alone I rambled up hills of broken stone.
Favoring the nooks of shade, lingering as I would.
Stood a while to mop my brow, maybe a while stood
Breathing deep and breathing deep in my laboring lungs.
Maybe, hurrying my pace, body forward flung
Panting hard and pressing hard on a thorny stick
In my right hand for support—like a shepherd's crook—
I went climbing for the heights, haunt of snatching birds
Native to the keener air—scuffing mountain herbs,
Sage and lavender and thyme, odors brash and sweet.
Over all the angry land fires of heaven beat.

A vulture on enormous wing at a lordly height
Sailed across the utter blue in its lonely flight.
In the distance one great peak blazing high and keen
And one low and rolling knoll, shield of damascene.
Many a lilac rise above leopard-colored ground,
Scraps of an old suit of mail thrown haphazard down.
Bare sierras far and wide. Duero, twisting river,
Draws a mighty crossbow back, to the full, forever
Rounding Soria: Soria, barbican to seal
In despite of Aragon the fortress of Castile.
Saw the far horizons were locked in mountain ranges
Crowned with oak—the evergreen or the oak that changes.
Naked areas of shale, scanty grass in these
Feeding the merino sheep; the black bull on his knees

In the verdure, ruminant; where the waters run
The brilliance of green poplars shone, in the summer sun.
Saw, without a breath of sound, travellers far away
—Shrunk to almost nothing, those!—horseman, driver, dray
Trail across the span of bridge; by its vaulted floor
Saw the waters turn to black that ran bright before.
Duero waters!

    Heart of oak where the Duero ran,
Old Iberia, Castile!

     Great and sorry land!
Land of the high wailing plain, waste of crag and crater;
Fields without a single plow, tree, or spurt of water;
Cities peeling tumbledown, roads without a tavern;
Yokels without song or dance, at a loss and sullen,
Who flee their homes as one might flee dying things—who
 flee
Even as Spanish rivers go pouring to the sea.

Castile so miserable now, and before so grand,
Wrapped in its rags and scorning all it scorns to understand.
Lagging, dozing, dreaming now? All that blood you poured
Forgot, when mightily you raged with fever of the sword?
All's turnabout: all flees and flows and runs in ravelling
 eddies—
Sea and mountain not the same, nor the eye that held them
 steady.
Vanished? And across the land a phantom moves, no more—
The ghost of folk who set God's flag victorious over war.

Mother who another time sent captains north and south
Is a poor mother now to grubs living hand to mouth.
Castile is not that noble land of centuries before,
When Myo Cid Rodrigo once, returning to Vivar,

In glory of new fortune and exuberant conquering
Gave all Valencia's fertile earth as keepsake to the king.
Not the Castile—when many a risk had proved its fervor
    true—
Could yearn to follow to the source the world-wide rivers, sue
For Indian kingdoms to the court, that mother of steel men,
Of warriors and commanders come laden back to Spain
Bringing in galleons of the king their gold and silver freight:
No hawk was keener for the kill, no lion for the fight.
Now syllogizing men, grown fat lapping pap of abbeys,
Scan the enormous firmament, eyelids hanging flabby,
And if they catch, as in a dream, certain distant whispers
Of uproar on the eastern quay, where furious seamen cluster,
Rarely care to shift a ham or yawn out, "What's the matter?"
Again the portals of the war go wide with iron clatter!

Castile so miserable now, and before so grand,
Wrapped in its scraps and scorning all it scorns to understand.

Low and lower now, the sun. From villages afar
A trill of bells is spilling soft chorals in my ear
—Now gather for their rosary-beads the grannies all in
    black—.
Suddenly two lissom mink glitter from the rock,
Look at me with jewel eyes, flash away, and come
Back at once—so interested! Darkening fields are dumb.
The tavern door is open now to where the road lies white:
Many a mile of lonely stone; overpowering night.

# CHRISTMAS BALLAD

*Del nacim.<sup>to</sup> 9.° R<sup>ce</sup>.*

San Juan de la Cruz

In time it came round, the time
ripe for the birth of a boy.
Much as a bridegroom steps
fresh from the chamber of joy,

arm in arm he arrived
entwining the sweetheart he chose.
Both in a byre at hand
the pleasant mother reposed

among oxen and burros and such
as the winter sky drove in.
How they struck up a tune, those folk!
Sweeter the angels sang!

There was a bridal to chant!
There was a pair well wed!
But why did he sob and sob,
God in his rough-hewn bed?

Such a dazzle of tears!—this gift
all that the bride could bring?
How the mother was struck at so
topsy-turvy a thing:

distress of the flesh, in God!
in man, the pitch of delight!
Pairs never coupled so;
different as day and night.

# SPANISH BALLAD

*¿Dó los mis amores, dó los?*
*¿Dó los andaré a buscar?*

Rose and went a-roving, mother,
On the morning of St. John.
Rose and saw a lass a-laundering
On the ocean sands alone.
Lone she wrings and lone she rinses,
Lone extends them on a thorn,
All the while the clothes are sunning,
Sings a solitary song:

"Where's my darling, where, I wonder?
How to wander where he's gone?"

Up the ocean, down the ocean,
Still the girl goes singing on.
With a gold comb in her fingers
For her tresses ocean-blown.
"You, you sailor, tell me truly,
True as heaven steer you home,
Have you seen him pass, my darling,
Seen him faring on the foam?"

# VII

*Lo jorn ha por    de perdre sa claror*
*quant ve la nit    que espandeix ses tenebres . . .*

# WHAT DAVID AND THE
# SIBYL KNEW

Apologize to the sea (if you can), to the chanting avenger.
Slip your guilt on the mêleeing sand. Clear yourself there.
  "Oh I've clouded your face, it's true.
  Cared nothing for you—"
Scan the pitching heaumes for a favor of love. Or at flair of
    danger
  Appeal to the air.

Tell all to the fair-lipped air (if you can), your bosom
    companion.
Crouched halfway up her exhilarant stair, blurt your black
    name.
  "Oh I've stricken the noon, it's true.
  Spread night-contagion too—"
Pose forlorn for a fawning of love. Or on eyries stranded
  Make for the flame.

Confess to the fire's torn heart (if you can), all ikon of
    anguish.
Tattle your dense and tepid art. Search it for worth.
  "Oh I've crippled your limbs, it's true.
  Stamped valor down in you—"
Reach meager palms for a fondling of love. Or at scent
    of menace
  Freeze to the earth.

And wheedle the tolerant earth (if you can), sweet-humored
    fellow.
String out like rags your carrion past. Orate your plea.
  "Oh I've blighted the June, it's true.
  Sickened a Yule or two—"
Feel round for a ferning of love. Or in pestilent meadows
  Retch for the faraway sea.

## ISAIAH'S COAL

*what more can man desire?*

Always, he woke in those days
With a sense of treasure,
His heart a gayer glow
Than his window grand with sun,
As a child, its mind all whirring
With green and hollied pleasure
Wakes in a haze of *Christmas*!
The season of secrets done.

Or as one on country linen
Wakes with a start one morning—
Then on comfort snugger than pillows
Floats: July at the lake.
Or has married a golden girl
And can hardly believe, but turning
Sees blossom for him that very face
Worshipping cameras take.

Toy trains whirr perky on
Till springs contort beneath;
The middle-age rower slumps
Like a sack—indignant seizure!
Late editions wail
*Screen Star in Mystery Death*—
Yet in those same days
He woke with a sense of treasure.

Knowing: my love is safe
Though the Rockies plunge like water,
Though surf like a wildfire rage
And omens roam the sky;

Though limbs of the swimmer laze
Pale where the seaweed caught her,
Nothing can touch my love
As dangerous time goes by.

# *DE FIDE*

### i.

I never saw one walk the sea—swing briskly off the land
As to a moving trolley car. And yet I understand.
I've walked it many times myself. Someone held my hand.

### ii.

Do you believe in Him? you ask. Safer to say No,
Since what I'd be admitting could be a death of snow,
Some hatchet whacks on an old log where pigmies slit the skin,
A Moses-beard, tremendous crag, or formulas of wind.
To these and maybe yours, it's No. But for another there—
You'd wonder, when I fill my lungs: Do you believe in air?

## LAST JUDGMENT

When we are ranged on the great plain of flabbergasting death,
Feeding (for our lungs hang slack) on air not drawn with
    breath,
And see, for many miles around, our Easter Island lie,
The gaping dumbshow of our shame, in footlights from
    the sky:
How many a scene long out of mind in rooms we barely knew,
Punch amok or Judy lewd, lit fuchsia-red or blue,
And see our working face in each and sway a moment numb—
Then save us from our rage Yourself; let lightning cry
    our doom!
Having such motive for their hate, each knowing what it
    knows—
We know our terrible hearts too well to trust our luck with
    those.

i.

They whitened at the privilege
Of tiptoeing near death
To watch his fingers skeining
Hand over hand the breath

From lips like violets blanching—
This taught a thing or two.
Their palms were mute; their faces
The shape of what they knew:

Something of love, whose eyes burn
Gayer with failing breath;
Of flesh, a dull conductor
Of nearly all but death.

Knowing, they shrunk closer
(The deadened with the dead)
When night drained of color
Drowsy aster-head.

Through that wound, the world lay
In extremis too:
Meadows wailed their mossy blood;
Heaven bled its blue.

ii.

"This flesh, a toy of death;
His cat-and-mouse display.
Tomorrow's numbing fall
Tense in the air today.

"A crazy frame, soon down,"
I grieved. But Love said, "Look!"

And the flesh soared and such
Wonderment took;

The eye so fine a star,
The cheek such mains of light
That "O Love, you appear
Unendurably bright!"

The sky glowed softly, "I?"
And marvelling, "*I* appear?"
Then all midheaven shone: "I
But set a finger here."

### iii.

The rose cajoling, "Now?"
The moon with shapely "Here?"
Persuaded. Waved away
The sheriff face of fear

Hardening, "Easy! *Here*'s
Bad acreage of *Where*.
And *Now*'s a fool mirage
Over coyote air."

"No, *Here*'s the attractive moon."
(The sheriff whacked his star.)
"And *Now*'s a garden dial
Where affluent roses are."

So once. No roses now.
No moon's ill-gotten glow.
*Here* shivers, "Far away?"
And *Now* weeps, "Long ago."

# CONCLUSION

*legato con amore in un volume*
*ciò che per l'universo si squaderna . . .*

If what began (look far and wide) will end:
This lava globe huddle and freeze, its core
Brittle with cold, or pulled too near its friend
Pop once like one gun in a long-drawn war,
And the stars sputter one by one, the night
So empty judging *empty*'s out of date
(Space and time gone), then only, height on height,
Mind that impelled those currents and that freight,
Mind that after five days (see those days!
Regions all tropic one day, one all ice!)
Whistled man from the sea-moss, saw him raise
The blundering forepaw, blink from shaggy eyes—
If image, likeness in the ox-yoke brow
Long out of focus, focused mind to Mind—
Ah what unspeakable two and two allows
That silence huddle and all eyes go blind?
Our ups and downs—there! that remembered makes
Memory which is the single mind. How sweet
Carmine stars of the maple fumed in rakes
At 1350 such and such a street.
A thing to keep in mind. Yes and keep yet
When both are one, the rose and violet.
Once in winter by the richening sill
Quiet, the fireplace tiny in our eyes—
I mention this; there's more. The Almighty will
Aeons late stumble on it with surprise.

# Knowledge of the Evening *

## POEMS 1950-1960
## by JOHN FREDERICK NIMS

John Frederick Nims has lived abroad nearly half of the decade in which these poems were written, mostly in Italy and Spain. It is not surprising therefore that many have their origin or setting in foreign places, nor that a number of the themes are European. Essentially the poems are, as he says, "about people I have loved and people death has claimed. Some are about things that came about at the wrong time or in the wrong place, or that never came about at all . . . but mostly they are about what poetry has always been about: about God and man, and whatever each seems to mean by the other; about love and death, eternity and time."